◄ THE GATEHOUSE HEAVEN ►

THE
GATEHOUSE
HEAVEN

POEMS
James Kimbrell

Winner of the 1997
Kathryn A. Morton Prize in Poetry
Selected by Charles Wright

Sarabande S Books

LOUISVILLE, KENTUCKY

Managing Editor
Sarabande Books, Inc.
2234 Dundee Road, Suite 200
Louisville, KY 40205

LIBRARY OF CONGRESS CATALOGING-IN-PUBLICATION DATA

Kimbrell, James, 1967–
The gatehouse heaven : poems / by James Kimbrell.
p. cm.
ISBN 1-889330-13-2 (cloth : alk. paper).—ISBN 1-889330-14-0
(paper)
I. Title.
PS3561.141677G3 1998
811'.54—dc21   97-27211
CIP

Cover Painting: Signorelli, Luca. *The Damned Cast into Hell.* Duomo, Orvieto, Italy.
(Detail) Used by kind permission. Credit: Scala/Art Resource, NY.

Cover and text design by Charles Casey Martin.

Manufactured in the United States of America.
This book is printed on acid-free paper.

Sarabande Books is a nonprofit literary organization.

For Jung Yul

◄ A C K N O W L E D G M E N T S ►

Grateful acknowledgment is made to the following magazines in which several poems in this collection are forthcoming or have previously appeared, some in slightly different versions:

The Antioch Review: "Rooftop"; *Country Journal:* "Allen's Lake," "Route's End"; *Gulf Coast:* "At Greers Grocery with Mrs. Thibodeau"; *Gulf Stream:* "Bongnae Mountain"; *Midlands:* "Late June Letter"; *The Nation:* "A Slow Night on Texas Street"; *Poetry:* "A Greeting," "Empty House," "The Gatehouse Heaven," "Memory," "On the Road above Jo-Yang Beach," "Orpheus in Yong Island," "Salvation," "True Descenders"; *Poetry East:* "Holiness," "Self-Portrait, Leakesville"; *The Southern Poetry Review:* "Mt. Pisgah," "Landing" (originally "The Trouble Now")

The stanza from Stéphane Mallarmé is from "Petit Air II," *Mallarmé,* trans. Wallace Fowlie. Chicago: University of Chicago Press, 1953.

The passage from Kusan Sunim is taken from *The Way of Korean Zen,* trans. Martine Fages. New York: Weatherhill, 1985.

I am especially grateful for a Ruth Lilly Fellowship from Ruth Lilly, *Poetry,* and The American Council for the Arts, which saw me through the writing of many of the poems included here. Thanks also to the Center for Writers at the University of Southern Mississippi, to the University of Virginia for a Henry Hoynes Fellowship, and the Creative Writing Program at the University of Missouri, Columbia.

◄ CONTENTS ►

Thornton Wilder once told an interviewer, according to J. D. McClatchy, "I am not interested in the ephemeral—such subjects as the adulteries of dentists. I am interested in those things that repeat and repeat and repeat in the lives of the millions." He meant, McClatchy goes on to say, the mysteries and marvels of the heart. Those things, I might add, that repeat and repeat in the individual life as well. One last Wilder quote—he once described Tolstoy as "a great eye, above the roof, above the town, above the planet, from which nothing was hid." This is the point of view James Kimbrell would take, and the recurring mysteries of the human heart are what he would look down upon through the poems of his compelling first book, *The Gatehouse Heaven*. Those mysteries that are hidden and unhandlable, the undercurrents that move us on, the undertow that takes us back in order to take us forward again, those forces that frame and format our lives, that filter and finish us.

And it doesn't take him long to focus and start boring in. The first poem in the book is called "Mt. Pisgah":

> It was the middle of the night and I had lived
> A long time with that country, with the hay
> Rakes and rock paths and the beam bridge
> Above the snake-thick waters. It was
> The middle of the night so far into the field
> The deer began not to notice the moons
> In the shallow bean row puddles. That's how dark

Fell over the road that led into town and kept us
All from moving. Still, when the train passed,
Milk shook in its bucket and the earth sank
In a little. So each year when the corn shrank
Back to stubble, the mud strewn with husks,
More than anything silence grew tall there
Between the kitchen window and the shed's
Roof and the one note rust made in the stuck
Weather vane, in the rooster holding north.

Now, Pisgah is a mountain in the Nantahala National Forest in North
Carolina. I once, at age 15, climbed to the top of it, and then, the next
morning, walked down and away from it for 45 miles, until 10 P.M. I'm
not at all sure this mountain has anything to do with that one. In fact, I'm
pretty sure it doesn't, as the walk to and from the place in Kimbrell's
poem seems much longer and darker than mine ever was. From the first
page, you know he's got his eye on you, as well as all the little and shining
things around you.

Gustave Flaubert, the White Knight of Normandy, once said that
everything in art depends on execution: the story of a louse can be as
beautiful as the story of Alexander. The title poem in Kimbrell's book is
the story—or part of the story, or, more likely, more than the story—of
his father's mental illness, and how it, as such things will, disrupted and
devastated not only Kimbrell himself, but his family as a whole and the
lives of everyone within it and tangential to it. A sad story beautifully
told, tough, poignant, and ultimately redemptive, both for the teller and
the main character. What is a language adequate to such a story? How
does one tiptoe along that razor's edge? Well, perhaps there are several
that might do the job. The one Kimbrell has is, it seems to me, not merely
adequate but often triumphant, that mixture of glittering surfaces and
glittering depths under the swiveling, probing eye. Here is a surface:

1976: He laid bricks despite the pills
    and doctor's orders. His hands
        steadied, chalky, caked with mortar;

the level, the trowel, the spool
of string, the endlessly unfolding
        measuring stick jutting out of his old
    blue bowling bag stationed beside
the front door. My father, doctor
    of fireplaces, fire walls, flower beds

    and red buildings that bricked out
the sky. He rested like a fed lion
        on the couch each evening with his cigarette
    and Old Milwaukee. But what
could anyone do when the weather changed?
        And it poured each day that late
    September. He flushed his pills. He cashed
his disability checks and burnt
        the umber envelopes marked "V.A."

And here is an undertow:

    His wing-tip shoes, his eyes,
his hands, the haircut
        he didn't like though it pleased
    the doctors—how far they were
from the angels and demons
        I staked around him

    that they might ward away
insanity which lit in the branches
        and weeds that lined the gates
    of the sanitarium. In white-
washed chairs that rocked
        like boats in a sea of pastel

    soup-can ashtrays, he talked
and smoked, and stared past

the hedges and picnic tables.
What was there to say?

There are ten, heartbreaking sections to this marvelous poem, each one different and etched, each one a layer of unknowing lifted and laid clear.

Flaubert again: "If you happen to write well, you are accused of lacking ideas." Well, Kimbrell, God knows, writes well. Here, for instance, are the first two and ⅖ths stanzas of a poem called "True Descenders," written after Luca Signorelli's *The Damned Cast into Hell:*

No matter how thunderous the chorus
   of their damnation, surely the wine-veined
gold-tipped fornicators must relish
some pleasure in the last hurling spiral
   down the spines of all the bat-winged devils.

Like the star-shaped sugar maple leaves
   plummeting toward the thick asylum
of my own backyard, that warped infinity
of roots, it's impossible that their descent,
   whether here or from the constellations

over Orvieto, could ever be anything
   other than beautiful, their harshly bronzed
breasts and buttocks growing more luscious
with every imaginable sin.

Believe me, after this gorgeous beginning, there are a couple of terrific ideas that come into play in the next page-and-a-half, running like quicksilver between Umbria and Jackson, Mississippi. And back again.

The craft is a serious one, and Kimbrell sings a serious song. Which is not to say he doesn't have an occasional self-deprecating side or whimsical moment. Witness the poem "On the Road above Jo-Yang Beach":

Half a mile up the mountain, wind swung the lanterns
That lined a temple and lit the path to a boat-sized bell.
How weightless, the life I imagined there, wordless
Days and few possessions. How unencumbered
Even memory would be freed of a home to return to:
No town I once knew, no hands quick to remember me
With an inch-above-the-steering-wheel wave. I'd
Heard the way to enter: refuse to leave until the monks
Consented. Pick a rock beside the gate and wait
For nights, weeks, for however many lives it might
Take to not backtrack down the mountain to a table
At a small restaurant, to not feel so nearly satisfied
As I did with oyster soup and a bottle of barley wine,
With the pining tremolos of Korean country music
And the sea wind chorusing over the corrugated roof.

Love of language, attention to detail, affection for what the eye sees
and the hands touch in the natural world, the desire to touch and see
what's beyond them (if only for an instant), the ache of longing for
something more permanent, less absent, the eventual assimilation of all
the loose threads of the heart into the mosaic of art, if not the outline of
one's own face (which is the same thing, as Borges tells us)—these are
the things James Kimbrell's poems both yearn for and personify at the
same time. I remember remarking to someone once, when asked about
picking up a new book of poems and what I looked for in it, that music
and substance were the first things. Brilliance in language, a language that
has a life of its own, seriousness of subject matter, a willingness to be
different, to take on what's hard and beautiful, a willingness to put the
hair shirt on and go into the desert and sit still and listen and write it
down. I also then said that this was probably asking too much. Now I'm
not so sure. This is a first book. The poems are deft and sure, there is a
sense of vision in them, and I have the feeling that this is the start of
something significant. And if, as Flaubert also said, language is like a
cracked kettle on which we beat out tunes for bears to dance to, while

all the time we long to move the stars to pity, then the stars have prime seating for these songs. Let's see what happens down the road. Like George Steiner, I've got my bet on transcendence.

Charles Wright
Charlottesville, VA
April, 1997

Voice foreign to the grove
Or followed by no echo
The bird one never heard
A second time in life . . .

—Stéphane Mallarmé
Trans. Wallace Fowlie

•

When both front and back are shattered
Then truly one has a complete mirror.

—Kusan Sunim
Trans. Martine Fages

I

Mt. Pisgah√

It was the middle of the night and I had lived
A long time with that country, with the hay
Rakes and rock paths and the beam bridge
Above the snake-thick waters. It was
The middle of the night so far into the field
The deer began not to notice the moons
In the shallow bean row puddles. That's how dark
Fell over the road that led into town and kept us
All from moving. Still, when the train passed,
Milk shook in its bucket and the earth sank
In a little. So each year when the corn shrank
Back to stubble, the mud strewn with husks,
More than anything silence grew tall there
Between the kitchen window and the shed's
Roof and the one note rust made in the stuck
Weather vane, in the rooster holding north.

A Greeting

It was natural to assume they too
would be drawn to the spired
    Southern Victorian grandeur
  we knew as haunted, but that drizzled-
under afternoon not a single
      soul spoke to our invocations
   dimmed to their séanced whispers,
not a wing-beat at the window
    . wisped out our candle with the bruised

    winds of the other world. Not even
for us, the still young enough
      not to disbelieve, would any breeze
   gathered in the gables croon
back through the indelible April mist
      of the dead. Had there been more
  than the shadows of branches
braided with moss, than the drip
   behind the mirrored mantel,

    more than the rush of trespassing
which set us afloat so far
    from those town-long fences and roads,
   what would we have said to any spirit
rowing in, its disembodied glow
      like a moon-splotched water filling
  the startled cups of our faces? For all
our desires to know, how could we
   have even begun to breathe

    in that visitation, in that room
gone to a flesh made air? Still,

though without the least speck
of luminescence, that failure
stirred the starless silence inside
      our orbit of hands, so that there
in the ghost midst of that absence,
in the untouched slumber
    of souls, all the portraitless nails,

the veils of dust, the walls
in their dun-colored lumber, seemed
     soaked, heavy as though to bar us,
   to keep us from swaying near,
as if just below the sloped
      wood floor a river had been
 flowing, trolling us away
from the hazy banks of the having lived,
    back toward the shore of the living.

Rooftop

Above the corner of Water and Seventeenth, when pigeons
Tapped the window and the mid-dusk light drew us out,
There was huge industry in the oncoming silence, in the print
Of darkness between low flight antennas and scattered
Cable dishes. The first quarter of moon over the bridge,
The last bend of river, and farther back, the trestle's web-work
Like an elbow above the trees, the entire town a foreground
For whatever we were after, something so close
We could see it disappear . . .
                                    But more than we cared
For the weedy mimosas or the bras on the lines or the iron
Gutter grates, more than the diesely tops of log trucks
Or the newspaper sheets stuttering through weeds in the field
Behind the school, it was the view above ourselves
That we wanted most to remember, and how easily we fell
Into feeling half-visible, level with the birds on the ladder
Of the silver water tower, with their angular winging away.

Wheels in August

It was all for a price, sweet summer wind, the highway's
Hash marks strobing through jags in the rust-cut floorboard.
And what could I do, after he piloted me at a hundred-
Thirty per up the river road in that souped Impala, the dash
Lit thick with the haze of his most righteous sinsemilla?
I was cruising around with a football star, a senior, but it
Was all in his drunk-hearted hope that evening with me

Came in exchange for the screen unhinged and laid
Aside in weeds beneath my sister's bedroom window. *Oh
She talks about you all the time.* How easily I lied,
As though pleasure impatiently awaited this almost man
I dreamed to become, taller like him, my voice un-
Naturally slurred, my flesh so blessed that were I to dive
From the Chickasawhay bridge the current would swell

A clear gulf blue, and all the girls on the sandbar
Would look up and see their mid-swan fantasy coming true.
But far too soon, I was fumbling in and out of my own
Home's kitchen door, stoned, ashamed by what my sister
Would say. How poised I sat beside him, feigning her
Denial, her flight to the unwakeable sleep where she reclined,
Beautiful, a novel of unfolding love unfolded facedown

On her nightgowned breasts. I knew all too well a lover
Withheld could be the larger life of desire, and though he
Was not my enemy, not my friend, that night in my high
Half-sleep, in those hours that seemed they never would
Give in, I heard his car rumbling by, a tap at her window,
Their whispers and laughter more careful and close
Than any lie that I would spin in my most jealous of dreams.

True Descenders ✓

—*after Luca Signorelli's* The Damned Cast into Hell
(remembered from a high school text)

No matter how thunderous the chorus
   of their damnation, surely the wine-veined,
gold-tipped fornicators must relish
some pleasure in the last hurling spiral
   down the spines of all the bat-winged devils.

Like the star-shaped sugar maple leaves
   plummeting toward the thick asylum
of my own backyard, that warped infinity
of roots, it's impossible that their descent,
   whether here or from the constellations

over Orvieto, could ever be anything
   other than beautiful, their harshly bronzed
breasts and buttocks growing more luscious
with every imaginable sin. And what's
   to be made of Saint Michael and his flock,

drawing their cloud-glazed swords,
   torsos wrapped in steel? Especially now,
when the landscape's flustered, it's difficult
not to begrudge the high archangel
   his stock of feathers, his cosmic lock

of windblown hair, his breastplate, cool
   to the touch. It's a point the leaves
don't have to argue, whether to give in
to the pull of a soon-to-be-iced
   patch of autumnal earth, or to resist and so hang

perpetually rigid, heavy-legged traitors
    to lust. Suppose our own innocence,
in that red November dusk at the end
of the world, should remain that righteous,
    should take up its silver armor against

the quicker passions ready to tumble
    in any celestial bed, we'd see how it is
that we've always lived in the house
of at least two Gods, one of nipples and random
    erections, one of devotion to the virtuous

invisible, and that to truly worship either
    is to finally love the other. If
the swollen, cartwheeling transgressors
of desire begin to desire once more,
    who'd not let the blue-with-death demons

untie their hands and follow their
    laughing down the hall? Who could
not feel their own body going holy?
Who would not take a lover then
    and guiltlessly watch the wrist-ropes fall?

Allen's Lake

It's the window I remember, and the moment
Before jumping to the woodpile and white grass.
It's the blue breath of palominos
And the swinging gable-light, the frozen stubble
Against my wrists each night I crawled
Under the gate. And once, where waves lipped

The rotted dock rafters, though I'd been warned,
I climbed out on the last slim beam
That jutted high across the water. Boots slick
Against the frost-crystalled edges, I tightrope
Stepped at least ten feet, and stopped there . . .
From that height, close to the star-bleared

Pine tips, I felt that lake take me into account.
I was another far object steeped
In the slow mist, a sound gathered together
Past a crooked beach of bank mulch
And snapped sticks, a catch
In the half-whistle of oaks. This was years

Before I'd seen how easily a body could get lost
In that mud-stumped, Hind's County cold,
Or how old saw-toothed boards
Are bridges over bones that sink
To the bottom of winter. I stood there,
Shivering, five minutes of luck, confident

That even falling could last forever. Arms scarecrowed
For balance, I listened in my careful
Backtracking to the wind

Tumble into a north-faced gust, white ribs
Of moon breaking on the water, one layer
Of light coming down,

                  one layer of light slipping under.

Late June Letter

—to K.O. on the North Shore

In my dream I was working toward the answer to all distance—
Around the corner, second blue house, there's a light
In the attic window. Across the street, a mockingbird's perched
In the pin oak branches. All the trucks
And tool trailers are parked in the long garage of the funeral home,
And behind it, Gordon's Creek, the sandpipers
Sweeping not two inches above
Two inches of water. I was trying to establish a balance—the flowers sleep,
The flowers bloom.

I was wondering if the world is what we think it is.
Around three each afternoon the katydids start shaking their maracas,
And the pines in their séance ignore us.
I can say we all have another shape—

I can say there is a squirrel carrying an acorn
To the altar. There is a boy asleep on the hay. There's a dark butterfly
Climbing the ladder. There's a trumpet
On the ground and the sky in a bucket of blue water.
There are the ghosts of three pigs holding hands, and the girl
Who hung her red hood on a birch twig.
She's letting the story go off by itself, she's swimming across the river.

Self-Portrait, Leakesville

The hay rake's rattle, the stunned sputter of a moccasin
Slung in the blades, the mid-gloam crickets sending
Their codes as though from a nearby country of dreamers.
Each sound found its shape—low drip into mud beneath
The leaking spigot, scrape of sparrows stowing twigs
In the eaves, the combines fading, unzipping the bean
Rows and back again, and the wind-combed drift
Of dust in the field, which is where I can hear it most
Clearly now, my pointing the direction away
From that town, saying *there I am, there I am, there I am. . . .*

II

The Gatehouse Heaven

"For the Father loveth the Son, and showeth him
all things that himself doeth: and he will show
him greater works than these, that ye may marvel."
—John 5:20

I

And what did I know of madness or fathers? First
The old gatehouse guard's country music, the katydids
And crickets and fire ants catacombed in their mirexed
Mounds. Then a narrow brick road and the groomed

Asylum lawn strewn with fronds of withering mimosas.
Then the fish-boned shadows of limbs, the walls
And barred windows awash in a light the color of rust,
Or river water, of a shade at dusk thicker than I'd seen

In the stain-glassed fields of junked automobiles
Jackson anchored to. After that, I thought it all saintly,
Heroic, the madhouse a heaven the farthest flung
Angels flocked in. And my father amongst them: gowns

And clouds and a ladder I climbed, rung by rung, hand-
Lengths behind them, far from the shock beds and Librium,
High above the wing-beats and wailing that filled
The halls he walked, his slippered feet testing the ground.

II

His wing-tip shoes, his eyes,
his hands, the haircut
    he didn't like though it pleased
    the doctors—how far they were
from the angels and demons
    I staked around him

    that they might ward away
insanity which lit in the branches
    and weeds that lined the gates
    of the sanitarium. In white-
washed chairs that rocked
    like boats in a sea of pastel

    soup-can ashtrays, he talked
and smoked, and stared past
    the hedges and picnic tables.
    What was there to say?
Madness pecked its way
    through the corners and towns

    and down the back roads
between the dots which I
    penciled in on the Grey-
    hound map: our house
and that hospital, two
    musical chairs we hovered

around, everyone anxious
to take their seat miles from him
        when the record stopped
        and the chemical chords
shook through his brain
        like a struck tuning fork.

As though to welcome
Him home from the long halls
Of pharmaceutical sleep,

Silence spread its cloth across
The dinner table, arranged
Itself in the bookshelves,

Stretched its shadow
Across the porch and perched
In the branches of the ever-

Greens. He moved in
An orbit between the bed,
An old Naugahyde chair

And the kitchen counter
Crowded with pill bottles.
And though he was there,

He was hardly aware
Of me when I sat down
Beside him, holding in

And letting go my
Breath in sync with his,
Staring as he stared

At the walls, at the cars
Which came and went
Along the road outside

The bedroom window, breeze
Lifting, breeze letting go
The white gauze curtains.

IV

Swimming past the creek shoals he turned
   into a bass into an eel into a father
      home again I climbed the ladder
         of his legs I held tight to his shoulders
            to the scent of sweat cigarette smoke

and the harsh sap of August pines
   which slipped back when we dipped
      down and shot through the water
         the silt-light wavering above he turned
            into a snake into a whale into a father

I fixed myself on the brink
   of breath face pressed to his back
      settled and ready to follow past
         webs of stump tangles of root oh dark
            thick with stars I was never afraid

of losing the shouts of children
   along the diving bluffs what I
      feared most was not holding on
         not staying under but letting go
            giving up my father for a mouthful of air.

V

1976: He laid bricks despite the pills
and doctor's orders. His hands
    steadied, chalky, caked with mortar;
  the level, the trowel, the spool
of string, the endlessly unfolding
    measuring stick jutting out of his old
  blue bowling bag stationed beside
the front door. My father, doctor
  of fireplaces, fire walls, flower beds

  and red buildings that bricked out
the sky. He rested like a fed lion
    on the couch each evening with his cigarette
  and Old Milwaukee. But what
could anyone do when the weather changed?
    And it poured each day that late
  September. He flushed his pills. He cashed
his disability checks and burnt
  the umber envelopes marked "V.A."

  He grew a beard and drank all day.
And though I hated the smell of autumn
    mixed with the empty cans
  and specks of vomit on the bathroom
floor, I let the front door swing
    with the wind, I turned up the radio,
  sang along and drummed
on the coffee table, knowing that he
  would rest in a house built of noise.

VI

It was the evening after my grandfather's funeral
That my father and I first drank together. That night
Behind the house we laughed and pissed as if
Death had freed up something in us, as if in lowering

That sky-blue coffin my father had descended into
The role of the eldest son, the dependable one
Graveside with all his brothers, well-dressed
And not weeping together. We sat beneath the moon-

Whitened maple branches toasting one another.
When he drank, I drank. I cussed when he cussed.
I crossed my legs. I bowed my chest. But when
He threw his glass as if to crack it against the lip

Of a star, when his syllables riddled over the tongue
Of some other man's wandering soul,
I sat there dumb. I couldn't reply. And what
Was there to say? I had already said good-bye.

VII

My mother filed divorce papers,
Sold the piano, boxed the pictures,
The forks and knives, cradled
The plates in old issues of *Spiegel*

And *The Clarion Ledger*. Off
We went, two hundred miles south
Of my father. Our new house:
A crooked white Victorian behind

Which grazed the landlord's cows.
And, behind them, a hilltop
Cemetery. I took my first job there,
Keeping the grass, placing

And replacing the pots and flowers
In that high garden of stones.
I felt the dead looking up
Through me as I stripped the leaves

Of vines with my hands. But what
I wanted them to see was nothing
Short of impossibility: my father
Sitting by the cemetery gates,

Talking to me about the shifting
Of the ground, and why
The new slabs buckled,
Why the winding brick

Sidewalk would never rest level
No matter how many weeds
I pulled, or how much grass grew
On the side of a red clay hill.

VIII

1996: In a dream I was shooting pool,
and there on the wall, between
       two bass shellacked mid-flail,
  an electric sign in full glow; not a tilted
can pouring a shimmering river
      of beer, but a book's gold

      jacket cover, and amidst a host
of neon praise, my father's name
      flashing on-off. How could I not
  have known? Had this been hidden
from me that I might not follow,
      that I might not become

      the boy who drowned on the heels
of a man whose shot sanity floated
      facedown on the water? I rushed
  from the bar and back to school
and pulled his book from a shelf,
      but when I read the words

      the words disappeared. I couldn't stop,
I wanted to know his story
      unfolding as I turned toward
  the end, all the pages gone blank
by then as if they had been
      the book of everyone's, of no one's life.

IX

Your father is here but you
   are the one driving him crazy
      he slips through windows wide
         as night he stands like an egret
            on puddles and fences we are

sorry he'll be here for a while he'll
   call if he needs some money
      your father has been hit by a car
         your father has had a stroke
            your father is bleeding from the roof

of his mouth is hovering above
   electric tables is a subject of study
      your father ran off the road
         in a rainstorm of stampeding deer
            your father was found sleeping

in a bank with the spangled music
   of multiple alarms we found him
      wearing this garbage bag don't
         you listen to him he does not
            know what he is saying.

X

I sat beneath the moth-stenciled halos, the hospital
    Yard-lamps. I studied the details, the decor of the temple gates.

I unfastened the tag worn there by the sane and waited
    For my father. First the nurse with her clipboard

And fulsome hello, and then he sat down beside me,
    His hand on my arm, his eyes combing the back-lit

Sweet gum limbs. He did not resemble the shadows
    Of freight cars crashing gently through trees.

He did not climb down from the moon, a dimly
    Audible music. He was not a snake shedding its skin

While the rats skittered along the boards in the webbed
    Corners of the landlord's shed. I've seen my father twice

In the past five years. Hitchhiking through,
    He phoned for a ride. What could I do? I took him

In a borrowed car the silent three hours to Jackson.
    And last Christmas he joked about his missing teeth

And laughed with his mouth closed. He could not
    Sit still, he shuffled with a cane down the road

And back again. When he calls I pencil his number in
    At the end of a dozen addresses.

And now, if I should want to speak to him, I'd have
   No idea where to go, though he is far from gone.

For years I've studied this picture of him
   Inscribed "London, 1951." One foot on the step

Of a gray stone building, he's smiling, his hair
   Slick and black, his slacks pleated, his shirt pressed

And buttoned to the top beneath a baggy cardigan,
   A book in one hand and the other held by a woman

Whose face is turned. Who is she? And where
   Is he going? Off-duty perhaps from the enlisted

Hangars, the Strategic Air Command, oblivious
   Then to the wailing sirens, the squadrons of paranoia

That would tail him long after I was born? It's quite
   The wonder, what madness can do for a man,

Much more than me far below the harsh light of heaven,
   Down here in the makeshift center of this world.

III

Landing

It has nothing to do with the clouds of the last sky,
Or the rain of this one, or the storm-glazed
Arrival in-between, which made, for a moment,
The world seem sudden, replete with all
The dilapidated walls and window-lit alleys
In the valley across Yong Island, this life
Disguised as the next. Nothing to do with the sound
Of the ocean through my window, with the trunk
Unpacked in the corner, with the salt smell
Of this night, or the crickets that trailed me
All the way from Virginia. It hardly seems relevant
Now that the women at the top of the loose
Stone steps speak a language I don't half know.
Even my radio, so adept at transmission, fluent
And oblivious, bleats out the message—again
You are *here,* again you understand so little.

The Pier

As though each wave from Tsushima to Pusan Harbor
   had lipped the hem of an angel's gown, as if
      the gulls were a jumble of syllables slingshot
         off the tongue of God, we praised the dinghies
         adrift beyond the bobbing squid-net buoys,

the passenger boats foiling in, the cargo liners
   so far away and in that haze wipe-offable. Little
      did we know that the more the June sun jalousied
         through that spiraled shell of sky, the more we'd find
         our own misgivings, that the hairline of horizon

wasn't so much the day slipping under
   as the blank border of vision, a few degrees
      beyond which, divine though it seemed, was yet another
         inlet lined with quays, a bay busy with sea-plant
         divers, their skyward plumage of flippers.

Sailors we were not. Nevertheless, worshipful,
   hell-bent, and perhaps, not altogether anchored,
      we took notes for that journey, how the umbrellaed
         oyster-eaters dotted the beach behind us, how
         the pre-dusk day-moon went under whitewashed

in a trellis of clouds, how what light there was
   was stippled within its own congregation, as
      it had been, and would be in the afternoons
         of a dozen other shores, in the sting
         of salt air, in the endless pavilions of mist.

A Slow Night on Texas Street

—Pusan, South Korea

After the dancing ended, and the Russians
Had boarded for Vladivostok, just then:
A kettle of water, a bottle of wine, a dimly
Audible scuffle of soldiers in the street,
Drunk in the middle of a cease-fire.

That was all that could be heard from the tables
And chairs, from the room with its mirrors
Vaguely aglow. No women in the corner
Selling drinks, no lonely GI mouthing
The words. A silence long enough to hold.

And then, as if it had never happened: music
Again, glasses touching, a couple hurriedly
Retaking the floor, the bartender shouting,
Counting his change, and someone writing
Someone's name in the breath-wet window.

On the Road above Jo-Yang Beach

Half a mile up the mountain, wind swung the lanterns
That lined a temple and lit the path to a boat-sized bell.
How weightless, the life I imagined there, wordless
Days and few possessions. How unencumbered
Even memory would be freed of a home to return to:
No town I once knew, no hands quick to remember me
With an inch-above-the-steering-wheel wave. I'd
Heard the way to enter: refuse to leave until the monks
Consented. Pick a rock beside the gate and wait
For nights, weeks, for however many lives it might
Take to not backtrack down the mountain to a table
At a small restaurant, to not feel so nearly satisfied
As I did with oyster soup and a bottle of barley wine,
With the pining tremolos of Korean country music
And the sea wind chorusing over the corrugated roof.

Salvation

It's not that I harbor a weeping willow
Shadow's worth of longing for those cloaked
    Turns and straightaways, or that swampy
South Mississippi was ever half as tragic
    As I dreamed it could be, but that I still cruise
From time to time in the dope-ripe
    Ford Fairlane of the mind where nothing
Has changed, where we remain hopelessly
    Stoned devotees of the TOWN OF LEAKESVILLE
Emblazoned upon the graffitied water tower's
    Testimonies to love. We believed speed
Would save us, would take us fast
    And far away from the junkyard wrecks
Stacked in their mile-long convoy to nowhere.
    And though losing the way should
Have seemed the worst of divine betrayals,
    We took it as a minor fall from grace,
Tail-spun over the embankment rail, rocking
    That flung steel body down as if to play
A barre-chord on the barbed-wire fence.
    I'll never know what angelic overseer
Was bored and on duty that night, but we
    Rose up and climbed out of the warped last
Breath of that car, no one with so much
    As a scratch on his head, not a drop
Of beer spilt, and the radiator hissing
    Like a teapot in hell when someone yelled
She's gonna blow! and each of us
    Standing there, starving for something more,
Something other than the back wheel
    Spinning that sudden dark, cricketed quiet.

Holiness

The paint has flaked off the warped boards
and shutters of the old house we lived in,
    and behind the backyard, bambooed
        and bear-grassed, the oyster-shell road
    winds to the cemetery, and the headlights

    glint on the granite stones. If this was home,
then home was where my own ghost hid,
    busy in the weeds of an undug plot, his
        divvied wishes coming true in the faintly
    salty, moon-whet arms of the town's

    most rebellious Pentecostal daughter.
How easily it comes back, his clumsiness,
    and her hips shimmied loose from a slip
        that smelled, unmistakably, of roses
    and sweat. And how they would never

    shine again after she was preachered
worlds from him, reborn with the gift
    of tongues. But that one mosquitoed
        August night, clothes shucked off
    in a makeshift pillow, they sprawled

    their hearts out and spread the good word
to the stars and vines, to the gates
    and staggered rows of markers,
        to the pines swaying in their skyward
    stations, oblivious, doomed and divine.

Bongnae Mountain

Early this morning the sixth
island appeared, rainy season
   lifting the mouth of Yongdo,
the ships moving no less
      slowly, no less eager to anchor,
   coasting in with a silence

   and dimension much larger than
their stay. There's a saying
   that came on the boats, "Enjoy
the trouble you can't escape,"
      which is why, I suppose,
   the women are picking weeds

   from the sloped onion rows,
why the dog is sleeping
   beside the man that mows
the grass with scissors, why
      wind swings the gate back
   and magpies glide over

   the fishnet fence. And though
I've not spoken today to any
      memory from home, no loblolly
angels laddering down these
      unhewn Asian pines, I'm
   bound as I ever was to the same

   one road, this wanting to watch
from a distance that never
      exists wherever I go. Even this
harbor's perpetual departure

is no kind of leaving at all,
is the last island coming

back, the unlinked trail
of ships tracing the thickest
inlet edges, hemmed against
the docks, the anonymous
chain-cranks and horns,
the bluest confines of water.

Orpheus in Yong Island

—at the Jo-Hwa Piano Institute

Heedless of score or metronome, he plays the harbor breezes—
   His clamor of hammered strings. Though some will argue
He's lost his way, his ivory keys scaled as if fed up
   With the fruits of harmony, it's impossible for bird or god
To flee his cacophony known all along the fish markets
   And cobblestones that sing the mountain down to the sea.
Each note is composed for cartloads of persimmons
   Or scarves, each bar bound to ship-sized clouds trolling
In their mismatched disarray. For each ear astounded,
   For every soul in the vicinity, his music weaves a round
Of days of hours which never stack up, which strut
   And scatter like pigeons at the wheels of the evening's
Last wagon—a skiff towed away from waves which seldom
   Roll in off-key, which seldom roll in on any key at all,
They crest and vanish so easily, pulling the ocean home.

IV

Return

Stellar as they are, the visual aches and ahs of Boston,
How not to wish for a day beyond travel, for a wave
In the eye of an esplanade telescope, its white crest
Splayed beneath the arc of a gull mid-dip and shouldered
As if on the stuck pendulum of an antique clock? How
Long might it last, time stilled in a still life hung
From the walls of the sky's museum? A truck's wind
Whips the awning, and the faux Doric portico landmarks
Our way to the room we've rented for yet another view,
The moon-glazed midnight roofs, the historic urban
Afternoons that we could hardly believe, the clouds
In bloom, the traffic, the sea,
            a blue pigeon feather caught in the eaves.

Route's End

There is no disappearance—I was told—least of all in winter,
Only passing, heaven, somewhere like the patchwork
Of breath that pockets a face in December. One morning,

When the 6:30 Bluebird bus geared up the cattle-gap, instead
Of meeting it, I took the board path into the barn behind
The ranch owner's lot. What I remember is how the motor's

Rumble cleared the hill, how the bus seemed louder
Because I hid from it. Even blackbirds that sat like clothespins
On the power line were heard best when they dipped, one

By one, back to branches. I poured a bucket of molasses
Oats, and in the frozen mud, beneath an old Appaloosa mare,
I dumped them. I climbed the dusty, spotted back, wrapped

My legs around the thick skin that twitched like an eyelid
Over sleep. Hooky was a form of half-leaving, a class-
Room full of faces going blank when the trio of syllables

Meant for me made the desk in the corner hold more light.
And though I was missing, I was there, someplace in the dark
And the hay-manure smell, the salt-scattering of light

Flecked through nail holes across the sheet metal like planets
Between the rafters, close constellations. If that horse
Had wanted to she could have launched me easily against

That sky of beams. I held to the mane. I barely moved.
This, I thought, was how the stars must see, unseen until
Their first slung strings of fire wedge in the strange luck of not falling.

Self-Portrait, Jackson ✓

The trees are hopelessly overstylized, the sycamores
And breeze-pulled willows, the live oak branches'
Groundward sprawl gracing the State Street mansions.
There's the hospital where I was born, and just beyond
The Jewish Cemetery, the manicured lawns where I
Was schooled in all the classical ways of feigning
Education. Strange how a place claims you, and doesn't.
How you wheel right in from past to present inside
A rented car, as if someone were waiting, an old lover
Perhaps, anxious to greet you, to be impressed, as if
That lover were the place itself. But home holds
No magnolias behind its back. And when you step
Into the parking lot all slicked up and wrong again,
Nothing welcomes you like the glint and glare between
Clouds which fail to arrange themselves, which loll
As they always have above their noon-cast shadows.

At Greers Grocery with Mrs. Thibodeau ◁

I saw her twice—in body and
in the tilted mirrors which doubled
the peppers and cauliflower
globular in staggered rows. How she
graced that store in her sundress
and sandals, turning an over-lit
fluorescence to a nearly

religious glow. She walked
worlds above my aisles of work,
my striped shirt, name tag and tie,
my hair in a regulation porcupinish buzz
up to the crown—I knew this wasn't me
but who else was there to be?
And what good would anything

short of metamorphosis do
given that she was thirty-two
and wed to the local hardware king?
If she brushed past the sugar-
bag pyramids, all Egypt bloomed
for me. If she waited by
the checkout stand I couldn't help

but think of the suite that we
would step into when we stepped
through the automatic doors. And yet,
whether I watched her weighing grapes
or checking various dairy dates,
what I wished most to know
was her outside my fantasy. I wanted

to turn without meaning to
and perhaps even say hello
while polishing apples
or misting the lettuce and never
once consider love or whatever
escape it was I imagined
love must bring. But that

was another dream which flew
miles away from being sixteen,
the clerk amongst clerks who
followed her out to the car, carried
her bags, and thanked her almost
inaudibly for the change
she carelessly let fall into my hand.

Memory

Even in the afterlife we worried about the end,
Too close to the cloud-walled home of the holy,
Our eyes gone cottony from the scrolled wind

Death was, our bodies hauled away from lovers
We could only understand through distance,
As if seeing through a dizzy glass-bottom boat

The stars and opened windows of rooms we once
Danced in, cast almost as poorly in our roles
As the ones who, by then, had taken our places.

Letters to a Vanishing Fiancée ✓

1.

The night you left I hooked my heart to that silver
Train's caboose, so to become, to be, if not
Together, at least passionately dismembered

There among the creosote ties and the rust-spiked
Rails that led, more and more, to you. How quickly
The past became a movie I fell salty-lipped and

Fast asleep in. How walking from that station
Was like waking in a theater, bewildered, the music
At a mawkish end. (What was that woman's name?

And who was the man she called "My Scientist"?
And why the telescope in the revolving door?
And what did she believe when she said she believed

In him? And why did that city look dark blue?)

2.

You loved me, you loved me not the moment
We split beside the Hudson. We had one map
To the gallery marked X, and two ways

Of arriving, apologetic, so famished
For one another that we would've laid down
On the wide marble steps were it not

For the bed of pigeon droppings. We took
The first thing agreed upon—the wrong
City bus. And though it drove us far from home,

How could we have argued, stunned
As we were by evening, by the pier pasteled
With dusk, our window-glazed reflections

Rising in the surface of each other.

3.

A momentary stay: that night, for instance, we slipped
Beneath the barrier chains, waltzed across
The viewing deck and assumed our table

At the abandoned café. If anyone had seen us
They would have known that we'd
Just made the grand decision to marry

No later than the fall. But the bay looked rugged
From that jagged height, and the moon nested
Like a hangnail hooked in the wind-bent trees.

And though we strolled through that darkness
As if through a curtain parted for applause,
If we'd not shown up to see our own appearance

It would hardly have existed at all.

4.

What we mistook for love was love replete
With silences we kept falling through.
Our first date: a failed attempt at biking. Our second:

A night at the planetarium, a heaven we couldn't help
But give in to once we'd reached your room;
Your dress draped on the chair-back, and cricket sounds

Bending through the window screen surrounded
The crooked space between my body and yours,
An absence which outlasted us. Such was our

Beginning, and such would be our end: two friends—
One adrift amidst the platform bustle, the other
Stepping into the passenger car's interior glow,

Glancing at the numbered seats, walking down the row.

My Father at the North Street Boarding House

The white brick steps were steep and off-level
Beneath the door which led to the door
Of his room. The half-hooked padlock knocked
As I knocked. A shuffling, then he led me
Into the curtained sunlight. The word
May not be flesh, but the voice is, and his
Had been marked and removed to keep cancer
From more than it had. We sat on his bed
With pen and pad. Through the window
I could see a window across from his, the high
Branches budding, the power lines and sky.

———

To not look at the cloth which covered his throat,
To not think of his voice, slurred or manic,
In summer mornings or late at night, in steady
Counterpoint with my mother, or with no one.
I'd driven two days rehearsing how I might say
That I loved him in a way that would not
Sound like I loved him despite miles of rivers,
Miles of towns where I was a kid without him.
He wrote and I spoke of daily things, the weather,
People he knew. There was the sound of a radio
Down the hall. One door, then another, closing.

The slight tap and scrawl of his pen across
The unlined paper. The room with gloam
Easing in, the lamp turned on in the corner.
I spoke, paused, spoke once more and said
Nothing I had wanted to. I stood there
Holding him. No sound then. No crickets.
No drunks stumbling in. Two grown men
Standing in a silence that did not fall apart
In the door's hinges, in the weeds beneath
My shoes, nor even when I heard it again
And again driving home through the April dark.

Empty House

Every few nights I walk over here, screen door opened
And springless, leaves now up to the second step,
No one watching out the window but me with my elbows
On the ledge, my face staring back at my staring in.

What if all along, I'd been waiting in there? What if
The bird left its nest behind the mantel and built
Another beside this glass? I still wouldn't know
How to read something so physical as any moment is,

Something as known as a crooked stick, as the look
Of one wing in the other. Maybe it's true that everything
Leads to this, a night in which silence displays its own

Hidden architecture, the hewn gables, the untranslatable
Syllable of moon in a tilt above the roof, only to show
How absent the self is. How picked of words. How near at hand.

Jennifer Eriksen

JAMES KIMBRELL

has been the recipient of a Ford Foundation Fellowship, a Henry
Hoynes Fellowship, and a Ruth Lilly Fellowship. He was twice winner
of an Academy of American Poets Prize, and has also received the
"Discovery"/*The Nation* Award, and *Poetry* magazine's Bess Hokin Prize.
His poems and co-translations (with Jung Yul Yu) have appeared in
journals such as *Poetry, The Antioch Review, The Quarterly,* and *Field.* He is
currently completing his Ph.D. in Creative Writing at the
University of Missouri, Columbia.